# Simplify and Thrive the Art of Downsizing and Frugal Living

## Table of Contents

# Chapter 1: Introduction

Welcome to "Simplify and Thrive: The Art of Downsizing and Frugal Living." In this book, we will explore the transformative power of simplifying your life and embracing frugal living principles. Whether you're looking to downsize your living space, reduce your expenses, or cultivate a more intentional and fulfilling lifestyle, this book is your guide to achieving these goals.

In the modern world, many of us find ourselves surrounded by excess—excess belongings, expenses, and commitments. This abundance can lead to stress, financial strain, and a lack of fulfillment. However, by intentionally simplifying our lives and embracing frugality, we can unlock a path to greater contentment, financial freedom, and a more sustainable way of living.

"Simplify and Thrive" is designed to provide you with practical strategies, insights, and inspiration to embark on your downsizing and frugal living journey. From decluttering your living space to reevaluating your spending habits, each chapter will offer actionable steps and thoughtful considerations to help you achieve your desired lifestyle changes.

Throughout this book, we will delve into the benefits of downsizing, the principles of frugal living, and the ways in which these practices can lead to a more meaningful and fulfilling life. We will also address the emotional and practical aspects of downsizing, offering guidance on navigating the challenges that may arise during this process.

Whether you're seeking to simplify your living space, reduce your environmental impact, or gain greater financial stability, "Simplify and Thrive" will empower you to take meaningful steps toward a more intentional and rewarding way of life. Let's embark on this journey together and discover the art of downsizing and frugal living.

Saving for retirement is a critical aspect of financial planning, and frugal living can be a powerful tool in this endeavor. By adopting frugal habits, individuals can free up more money to put toward retirement savings. Living frugally in retirement involves applying the principles of frugal living to your post-career years. Living frugally can be a great way to save money and live more simply. It often involves making thoughtful decisions about spending, such as prioritizing needs over wants, finding ways to reduce expenses, and being mindful of one's consumption. Many people find that living frugally not only helps them save money but also leads to a more sustainable and fulfilling lifestyle.

Frugal living is a lifestyle focused on mindful spending and resourcefulness. It involves making deliberate choices to minimize expenses, avoid unnecessary purchases, and maximize the value of every dollar spent. Frugal living can encompass various aspects of life, including budgeting, meal planning, minimizing waste, adopting do-it-yourself practices, and seeking out discounts or secondhand items. While frugal living often involves cutting back on certain expenses, it isn't solely about deprivation; it's about prioritizing what truly matters to you. Many people find that frugal living not only helps them save money but also reduces stress and encourages a simpler, more meaningful way of life.

Frugal living often encourages people to prioritize their spending on things that truly add value to their lives, such as experiences, relationships, and personal development, rather than on material possessions. It can also lead to a greater sense of self-sufficiency and creativity, as individuals often find innovative ways to meet their needs without overspending.

# Chapter 2: Why Frugal Living

Frugal living is not merely about pinching pennies or deprivation; it's a deliberate and mindful approach to managing our resources, prioritizing what truly matters, and aligning our spending with our values and goals. From achieving financial independence and reducing stress to minimizing environmental impact and aligning spending with personal values, we uncover the diverse motivations behind this lifestyle choice.

People choose to embrace frugal living for various reasons. Some do it to achieve financial independence, pay off debt, or save for long-term goals such as retirement or travel. Others are drawn to frugal living as a way to reduce stress and find contentment in a simpler lifestyle. Many see it as a means to minimize their environmental impact by consuming fewer resources and creating less waste. Additionally, some people may adopt frugal living principles as a response to a change in circumstances, such as a job loss or unexpected expenses. Living frugally in retirement also involves making conscious choices to stretch your financial resources and live within your means. Ultimately, frugal living can empower individuals to take control of their finances, minimize their ecological footprint, and align their spending with their values and priorities. This doesn't have to be a difficult task, but it is necessary in today's economy.

Frugal living can help retirees maintain healthier financial situations, especially if unexpected expenses arise. By being mindful of their spending and embracing simplicity, retirees can be better prepared to navigate potential financial challenges in retirement.

Why I chose to live a more frugal life was due to inflation. I had already done a lot of cutting back on my spending but when inflation of 2023 hit my income was not going to be enough to sustain my spending habits. So, since the prices were going to drop, I had to curb how I spent my money. I had to create a budget that was going to fit all my needs then my wants. Creating a realistic budget that aligns with your retirement goals. Regularly review and adjust the budget as needed to ensure financial sustainability. This was the hardest part because I love Hello Kitty and I wanted to buy every item of it I had seen. Also, my love for wine had to be within that budget. In the beginning it was buy one sell one or give one away as a gift. So, if I buy an item, I have to either sell an item or give an item away. I started giving away a lot of shoes first. I didn't wear high heels shoes much anymore, so I cleared my closet of those first. I kept a few just for life happenings such as weddings and funerals. All the clothes were the next thing in line. I saw this system somewhere that if you didn't wear it in over a year then you weren't ever going to wear it again so donate it. This was the second hardest part because like many other people we think we're going to fit those jeans again one day when we lose weight or get back in shape. But that never happens. I love to eat but like to eat healthily.

If you develop a comprehensive budget that outlines your income, expenses, and savings goals and regularly review and adjust your budget to ensure it reflects your current financial situation you will find that it does get easier. It just takes a bit of time. Eliminate unnecessary expenses by using coupons and try to take advantage of sales to stock up on your daily use items.

We really weren't big on eating out at restaurants. We had stopped that long time before retirement, but you can limit the number of visits to local restaurants by cooking more meals at home. We also use intermittent fasting a few times a week. We learned to cook our favorite meals at home. It also gave us something to do together.

We both drove separate vehicles although we worked in the same general area, we had separate hours and overtime gave us more money but not much time spent together. So, upon retirement we donated one car and the one car we shared but we did most things together. As my mother-in-law said, "we were joined at the hip". So, cutting back on the number of vehicles we had was easy. Plus, it cut our insurance bill down a lot.

Embracing this new way of living in retirement can reduce financial stress and provide a greater sense of control over one's finances. This can lead to a more relaxed and fulfilling retirement experience. Frugal living encourages retirees to be resourceful and find innovative ways to meet their needs without overspending. This mindset can be especially valuable in retirement, where finding cost-effective solutions and making do with less can help stretch financial resources. Frugal living aligns with principles of sustainability, and retirees often find that living more simply and consuming fewer resources not only benefits their finances but also has a positive impact on the environment.

Embracing frugality in retirement can lead to a greater appreciation of life's simple pleasures. Retirees often find joy in activities and experiences that don't require significant spending, fostering a sense of contentment and fulfillment. While living frugally in retirement can support financial stability and a more satisfying lifestyle, it's essential to strike a balance and ensure that frugality doesn't detract from well-being and enjoyment. Retirees may find a sense of fulfillment in purposefully spending on experiences that bring them joy and fulfilling their personal goals while still adhering to frugal values. Whether you're seeking financial stability, a more sustainable lifestyle, or a deeper sense of purpose, the "why" of frugal living sets the stage for the transformative journey that lies ahead.

Join us as we explore the compelling reasons behind frugal living and discover how it can pave the way for a more intentional and rewarding way of life.

## Chapter 3: How to Start

Define your retirement goals and estimate the amount of money you'll need. Consider factors such as living expenses, healthcare costs, and any desired lifestyle choices. Living a frugal life involves making conscious choices to prioritize needs over wants, avoid unnecessary expenses, and make the most of available resources. Frugality can lead to financial stability by helping individuals save money, reduce debt, and build a financial cushion. This can provide a sense of security and peace of mind, especially in times of economic uncertainty. A frugal lifestyle often involves avoiding unnecessary debt and focusing on paying off existing debts. By living within one's means, individuals can work towards becoming debt-free, which can lead to increased financial freedom.

Frugal living is often associated with a focus on sustainability. By consuming less, individuals reduce their environmental impact and contribute to a more sustainable lifestyle. This can include practices such as recycling, reusing items, and minimizing waste. Frugal individuals prioritize saving money for future goals, emergencies, or retirement. This disciplined approach to saving can provide a financial safety net and enable individuals to achieve their long-term objectives.

Financial stress is a significant concern for many people. Living frugally can help reduce stress by providing a greater sense of control over one's finances. Knowing that you have savings and are not burdened by excessive debt can contribute to overall well-being. A frugal lifestyle encourages individuals to evaluate their priorities and focus on what truly matters to them. This can lead to a more fulfilling life by emphasizing experiences, relationships, and personal growth over material possessions.

By avoiding unnecessary expenses, individuals may have more flexibility in their choices and experiences. This could include the ability to pursue non-traditional career paths, take sabbaticals, or retire earlier than planned. Frugal living encourages mindful consumption and a critical evaluation of purchases. This mindset can lead to more intentional and fulfilling spending, avoiding the trap of excessive consumerism. Having a frugal mindset often involves preparing for unforeseen circumstances. By maintaining an emergency fund and avoiding unnecessary expenses, individuals are better equipped to handle unexpected events like medical emergencies or job loss.

The process of living frugally often requires discipline, creativity, and problem-solving skills. Overcoming challenges and finding alternative, cost-effective solutions can contribute to personal growth and a sense of accomplishment. It's important to note that frugality is a personal choice, and what works for one person may not work for another. The key is to strike a balance that aligns with individual values, priorities, and financial goals.

# Chapter 4: Financial Stability

Aim to enter retirement with minimal or no debt. Reducing or eliminating debts before retirement can significantly alleviate financial stress. Frugal living often involves prioritizing debt repayment, including mortgages, credit card debt, and student loans. By reducing or eliminating debt before retirement, individuals can enter their retirement years with fewer financial obligations and greater flexibility. If you have credit cards use your cashback rewards towards your bill or use them to pay off another debt you may have.

Financial stability refers to a state of financial well-being in which an individual, household, or organization has the capacity to meet their financial obligations, withstand financial shocks or unexpected expenses, and pursue their long-term financial goals. It encompasses the ability to manage day-to-day expenses, save for the future, and withstand economic uncertainties without experiencing significant hardship. Financial stability is closely tied to the relationship between expenses and income. By effectively managing expenses, living within one's means, and maximizing income through prudent financial decisions, individuals can work toward a state of financial well-being that supports their current needs and future aspirations. Creating and adhering to a budget is a fundamental tool for managing expenses and income. A well-structured budget allocates funds to essential expenses, savings, debt repayment, and discretionary spending, providing a clear overview of one's financial situation.

Achieving financial stability involves ensuring that income consistently exceeds expenses. This allows individuals to cover essential costs, save for the future, and build a financial cushion. It also provides the flexibility to address unexpected expenses and pursue long-term financial goals.

Explore various sources of income, such as Social Security, pensions, annuities, and part-time work. Diversifying income streams can provide added financial stability. I started my hot sauce business and gardening for growth as well as an added income. Selling to neighbors, friends and local markets helps create our emergency fund. This helps with any housing expenses that may arise. You know the ones were never prepared for. A financially stable entity typically has a reliable source of income that covers its regular expenses. This balance ensures that there is a surplus to save or invest in future needs.

You can start by writing down all your expenses. From there decide which ones are a necessity. These are the necessary costs of living, such as housing, utilities, groceries, transportation, and healthcare. Essential expenses are non-negotiable and form the foundation of a household's budget. Next write down all your discretionary expenses. These are non-essential expenses, such as dining out, entertainment, travel, and luxury items. While discretionary expenses can enhance quality of life, they are the areas where individuals have the most flexibility to adjust their spending. You can be flexible on these. But cutting back on these are necessary to live a frugal life. What are your fixed expenses. Your rent/ mortgage, and insurance. Now all your variable expenses should be listed. These are costs that fluctuate from month to month, such as groceries, utilities, and entertainment. Managing variable expenses effectively is important for maintaining a balanced budget.

Now let's get to your income. This is the part that helps you create and balance your debt and help you better budget your expenses. What is your primary income? This is the main source of earnings for an individual or household, typically derived from employment or self-employment. It forms the basis for meeting essential expenses and saving for the future. This is your retirement income. This income will only go up every few years or so. This should be used to pay your housing expenses as well as to pay into your emergency fund. Secondary income includes additional sources of earnings beyond the primary income, such as income from investments, rental properties, freelance work, or side businesses. Secondary income can provide financial flexibility and contribute to long-term financial stability. Now this income can be used for investing in your future.

There are many ways to enhance your monthly income, to pay down debt and to pay your variable expenses such as your gas and light bills. Utilizing your cashback credit cards or your rewards cards for everyday purchases can help offset variable expenses. These cards offer cashback, points, or any other rewards for qualifying purchases, effectively providing a form of reimbursement for spending.

Leveraging discount and coupon websites can help reduce the cost of variable expenses. Whether it's finding discounts on groceries, entertainment, or dining, these platforms provide opportunities to save money on everyday purchases. Joining loyalty programs offered by retailers, restaurants, and service providers can lead to discounts, freebies, and exclusive offers. Accumulating points or rewards through these programs can be used to offset variable expenses. Take advantage of cashback and rebate offers provided by manufacturers or retailers. This can result in savings on your purchases. These offers may be available for groceries, household items, and other variable expenses.

Acquiring gift cards through promotions, rewards programs, or discounted gift card marketplaces can be a way to prepay for variable expenses at a reduced cost. Using gift cards for everyday purchases effectively reduces the out-of-pocket expense for these items. Some companies offer referral or affiliate programs that provide rewards or cash incentives for referring new customers or making qualifying purchases. By participating in these programs, individuals can earn rewards that can be used to offset variable expenses.

By leveraging these alternative means to pay for variable expenses, individuals can effectively reduce the out-of-pocket cost of everyday purchases, maximize savings, and potentially free up funds for other financial priorities. It's important to approach these strategies thoughtfully and responsibly, ensuring that they align with one's overall financial plan and goals.

Various cashback apps and websites offer rebates or cashback on purchases made at participating retailers. By using these platforms for everyday shopping, individuals can earn cashback on groceries, dining, and other variable expenses. There are apps you can use to help you earn money just buy snapping picture of all your receipts. I use Receiptpal, Receipthog (code: mol73502), Coinout, and the last one is Fetch rewards. They are so easy all you do is open the app join and snap pictures of all your receipts. Points add up and they offer gift cards to a number of places. I also joined Clearvoices surveys, and this app gives you Amazon gift cards only. YouGov is an app that gives gifts cards as well as cash. Once you hit over 100,000 points you can cash put up to $100. Or keep going to cash out larger amounts. You can choose to get cash through PayPal. I start every year in November and by the time Christmas the following year comes around I have enough cash and gift cards to get my sons something for Christmas. This is a great way to not use my income to buy their gifts. I also use the apps to get things I need around the house or for my pets and garden. You can also pay bills doing it this way. This is all part of my budgeting practices.

Financial stability is not a one-size-fits-all concept; it varies based on individual circumstances and goals. It requires ongoing attention, adaptability, and a commitment to sound financial practices.

# Chapter 5: Eliminating Debt

There are many ways that you can start eliminating your debt to become financial free. First you need to get money smart. Choose a debt repayment strategy that suits your preferences. The debt snowball method involves paying off the smallest debts first, while the debt avalanche focuses on the highest-interest debts.

If you choose to use one of those agencies that help you with your debt and credit repair, they will use the debt snowball. Fist they will have you cut all your credit cards. They will call all your creditors and negotiate a lower amount by taking off pennies on the dollar which is just the interest on the total balance owed. Then they will have you pay them an amount that will cover the monthly cost of paying your debt as well as their fees for helping you.

Debt elimination can be done for free by using the snowball method yourself and you get to keep all your credit cards. The snowball methods are an easy way to eliminate or lower your debt in a fast and easy way. The debt snowball method is a debt-reduction strategy where you pay off debt in order of smallest to largest, gaining momentum as you knock out each remaining balance. When the smallest debt is paid in full, you roll the minimum payment you were making on that debt into the next-smallest debt payment.

There are also websites you can use to help decide how much more money you will need to pay down your debt. WalletHub and Credit Karma are both great ways to keep you informed on your credit history. They both offer free access to credit scores and reports from TransUnion. Credit Karma also uses Equifax. Users can monitor their credit profiles and receive alerts about changes. There are many things to consider when using these sites. While these platforms provide valuable credit information, it's important to note that the credit scores they provide may differ slightly from the scores the lenders use. Users should prioritize the security of their personal and financial information when using these platforms. Both WalletHub and Credit Karma implement security measures, but users should follow best practices for online security. Users may prefer one platform over the other based on additional features, such as tax preparation, insurance tools, or specific financial education resources.

List all your debts, including the outstanding balances, interest rates, and minimum monthly payments. This provides a clear picture of your overall debt. Differentiate between high-interest and low-interest debts. High-interest debts often warrant prioritized repayment. Understand where your money is going by tracking your monthly expenses. Identify areas where you can cut back to allocate more funds toward debt repayment. Develop a budget that aligns with your financial goals. Allocate a significant portion of your income toward debt repayment while still addressing essential expenses. While focusing on the prioritized debt, continue making minimum payments on other obligations to avoid penalties.

Explore opportunities for additional income through part-time jobs or side hustles. Allocate this extra income toward debt repayment. As you declutter your home you can take those items and sell them to help pay down your debt.

Reach out to creditors to negotiate lower interest rates. Explain your situation and emphasize your commitment to repaying the debt. Explore balance transfer options to consolidate high-interest debts onto a single, lower-interest credit card. Be mindful of transfer fees and introductory rates. They may opt to lower your interest rate for a period of time to allow you time to catch up and also build your credit at the same time.

Celebrate each debt paid off as a significant accomplishment. Recognize your efforts in working toward financial freedom. As you make progress in repaying existing debt, resist the temptation to accumulate new debt. Practice responsible financial habits to prevent backsliding. This doesn't mean going out and spending money. Rely on your emergency fund for unforeseen expenses rather than turning to credit cards. You can use this to help educate yourself more in finances.

Planning for your future so once you've eliminated your debt, redirect the funds you were using for repayment toward savings and investments. Plan for long-term financial goals and build wealth.

Eliminating debt requires commitment, discipline, and strategic planning. By assessing your debt situation, creating a realistic budget, prioritizing high-interest debts, and seeking additional income, you can make steady progress toward becoming debt-free. Remember that the journey to debt elimination is a gradual process, and staying focused on your financial goals will lead to greater financial stability and peace of mind. Once you've eliminated your debt, redirect the funds you were using for repayment toward savings and investments. Plan for long-term financial goals and build wealth.

## Chapter 6 Investing

Educate yourself in personal finance, budgeting, and investing. Understanding financial principles empowers you to make informed decisions and plan for the future. Many people adopt frugal living to achieve specific financial objectives, such as paying off debt, building an emergency fund, buying a home, or funding their children's education. By being intentional with their spending and cutting back on non-essential expenses, individuals can accelerate their progress toward these goals. Financial stability in retirement is a crucial aspect of a person's overall financial plan. Retirement planning involves saving and investing during one's working years to ensure a comfortable and secure lifestyle during retirement.

Saving for retirement is a critical aspect of financial planning, and frugal living can be a powerful tool in this endeavor. By adopting frugal habits, individuals can free up more money to put toward retirement savings. Start saving for retirement as early as possible. The power of compounding allows money to grow over time, and starting early gives your investments more time to increase in value. A few things you can do is to increase your savings. Frugal living often involves spending less on non-essential items, allowing individuals to allocate a higher percentage of their income toward retirement savings. This can accelerate the growth of retirement accounts such as 401(k)s, IRAs, or other investment vehicles.

If you retire early as I, did you can minimize expenses and maximize your savings, some people are able to achieve financial independence at a younger age. Also, smart investing can help you save for early retirement and also follow even after you retire. You don't have to wait until you retire to invest.

Diversify your investment portfolio to manage risk. A well-diversified portfolio can include a mix of stocks, bonds, and other assets to help balance potential returns and volatility. Robinhood is a cell phone app that can help you manage your portfolio and teach you how to invest in stocks and other things. They beat the banks on annual percentage rates as well as IRA's. You can simply open your account and start investing. Robinhood gold can boost your retirement with a 3% match on your contributions. You will also get 5% APY with your gold account. As well as roundups where you can buy a cup of coffee for $2.50, and your round cost would be $3,00 which the $0.50 can be invested towards any stock of your choosing. It's just that simple.

Spread your investments across different asset classes, such as stocks, bonds, real estate, and commodities, to reduce risk. Diversification can help protect your portfolio from the negative impact of a single investment's poor performance.

Instead of investing a large sum of money at once, consider using a dollar-cost averaging strategy. This involves investing a fixed amount of money at regular intervals, regardless of market conditions. This approach can help smooth out the impact of market volatility on your investments.

If you invest in dividend-paying stocks or funds, consider reinvesting the dividends to purchase additional shares. This can help accelerate the growth of your investment portfolio over time. Keep yourself updated on market trends, economic indicators, and the performance of your investments. Understanding the factors that influence the markets can help you make more informed investment decisions.

Regularly review your investment portfolio to ensure that it aligns with your financial goals and risk tolerance. Rebalance your portfolio as needed to maintain the desired asset allocation.

Be mindful of the tax implications of your investments. Utilize tax-advantaged accounts such as IRAs and 401(k)s and consider tax-efficient investment strategies to minimize the impact of taxes on your investment returns. If you're unsure about investment decisions or need guidance on complex financial matters, consider consulting with a financial advisor or investment professional. They can provide personalized advice based on your financial situation and goals.

Look for opportunities to invest in companies that produce sustainable products and services, such as eco-friendly consumer goods, organic food, and ethical fashion brands.

Consider impact investing, which focuses on generating positive social and environmental impact alongside financial returns. This can involve investing in projects or companies that address issues such as poverty alleviation, sustainable agriculture, or affordable housing.

Explore investments in sustainable real estate, such as green buildings, energy-efficient housing developments, and properties with environmentally friendly features. These investments can contribute to reducing carbon emissions and promoting sustainable urban development.

Healthcare is the biggest part of retirement and frugal living. Consider healthcare costs in your retirement plan. With costs on the rise living frugally helps cover healthcare costs. Also consider changing how you eat and exercising more to gain better control of your health. Medicare typically covers some health expenses, but additional insurance or savings may be necessary for comprehensive coverage. When considering long-term care insurance, individuals should carefully review policy details, compare options from different insurers, and assess their own financial situation and potential long-term care needs. It's often advisable to plan for long-term care well in advance to secure coverage when it's most affordable and accessible. Consulting with a financial advisor or insurance professional can provide valuable guidance based on individual circumstances.

When discussing your long -term insurance your coverage is the most important part of your insurance. LTCI typically covers a variety of long-term care services, including assistance with activities of daily living (ADLs) such as bathing, dressing, eating, and using the bathroom. It may also cover services provided in a variety of settings, such as at home, in an assisted living facility, or in a nursing home. The benefits provided by long-term care insurance can help pay for the costs associated with long-term care, which can be substantial. This may include the cost of home care aides, assisted living facilities, nursing homes, and other related services. To qualify for long-term care insurance, individuals usually need to meet certain health requirements. The underwriting process may involve a review of medical history and may include medical exams or health questionnaires. It's generally easier to secure coverage when one is in good health.

The cost of long-term care insurance premiums can vary based on factors such as age, health status, the amount of coverage, and the length of the benefit period. Premiums are typically lower when individuals purchase coverage at a younger age. However, there is a waiting period before your benefits are paid. This is called the elimination period. During this time, you are responsible for your own coverage. Given the rising cost of healthcare, some long-term care policies offer inflation protection options. This helps ensure that the benefits keep pace with the increasing costs of long-term care services.

Long-term care insurance policies come with various design options. These include the daily or monthly benefit amount, the benefit period (how long benefits will be paid), and any additional riders or features. It's extremely important to be aware that certain government programs, such as Medicaid, may provide coverage for long-term care services for those who meet specific financial and eligibility criteria. However, Medicaid is a means-tested program, and individuals may need to spend down their assets to qualify.

## Chapter 7: Downsizing

Downsizing is often driven by a desire for simplicity, financial considerations, or changes in lifestyle. It's important to approach downsizing thoughtfully, considering both the short-term and long-term implications. Additionally, if you own a business, it's crucial to manage the process with sensitivity to the impact on employees and the overall organizational culture. Whether downsizing housing, possessions, or business, the goal is often to achieve a more focused and efficient use of resources.

Evaluate housing needs during retirement. Downsizing or relocating to a more cost-effective area can free up resources and reduce living expenses. Downsizing our home was at first nothing we had ever thought about since it was our first home we bought and raised our children in. After they all grown up, we didn't need that much space. What we really wanted was a lot of land for growing our garden on a bigger scale. It was something that we decided to do to curb our food bill. We looked for housing in other places and decided that we wanted to live in Kentucky. They had a lot of houses the fit our lifestyle and the land that we wanted. As an added gift there was peace and quiet.

As an empty nester you may want to think about downsizing your housing to a more manageable size. This can also help reduce maintenance costs and property taxes.

As a retiree you may want to consider downsizing to a smaller home or a retirement community. This can free up equity tied to a larger property and reduce the physical demands of maintaining a larger residence. There are many options. Assisted living facilities for residents who require assistance with daily activities, such as bathing, dressing, or medication management. On the flip side of that there are independent living units, such as apartments, condos, or single-family homes, are common in retirement communities. These units are designed for seniors who can live on their own but prefer a community with peers. CCRCs provide a continuum of care, offering independent living, assisted living, and skilled nursing care on the same campus. This allows residents to transition to higher levels of care as their needs change.

The amenities and services vary among the communities you choose. There are 55 and over communities that have recreational facilities with fitness centers, swimming pools, golf courses, and walking trails. These are your higher end communities.

Social activities within the community are well organized including clubs, classes, and events to foster a sense of community and help you stay engaged. There on onsite dining areas or you can have your meals =provided for convenience. Healthcare services such as wellness programs, and access to medical professionals to support all your health and wellbeing needs.

Most of these communities are in a safe, secure, and monitored environment. This will provide you with a sense of peace. They have gated entrances, security personnel, and emergency response systems in place. Living in a retirement community often involves monthly fees, which can cover services, amenities, maintenance, and other community expenses. It's essential for residents to understand the fee structure and any potential additional costs. Entrance fees are common in CCRCs, where residents pay an upfront fee in addition to monthly fees. This fee is often partially refundable or may cover future healthcare needs.

Retirement communities are situated in various locations, from suburban settings to more urban environments. The location can influence the lifestyle and access to nearby amenities and services. Some retirees choose to move to a retirement community in a different region or climate for a change in lifestyle or to be closer to family.

Prospective residents should carefully review contracts and legal documents associated with the retirement community, including residency agreements and any provisions related to healthcare services. Understanding the terms and conditions, as well as any potential exit or refund policies, is crucial when considering a move to a retirement community.

Downsizing can be emotionally and physically demanding. Seek support from friends, family, or professional organizers to help you through the process and provide encouragement along the way. Make sure you clearly define your reasons for downsizing. Whether it's to reduce expenses, simplify your lifestyle, or prepare for retirement, having clear goals will guide your downsizing process and help you stay focused on what's most important to you.

# Chapter 8: Decluttering

I had always been told that space and time needs to be filled. But they didn't say much about the clutter that is involved with that. As well as all the dust and cleaning that is involved with all clutter.

Downsizing often involves decluttering your living space and sorting through your belongings. Determine what items you want to keep, donate, sell, or discard. This process can be emotionally challenging but is essential for downsizing effectively.

This can help you generate extra income, reduce the number of belongings you need to move, and benefit others in the process. Holding garage sales as well as posting them on social media sites. Craigslist is a good option as well. But as with all things be careful and have people there by your side to help you navigate through difficult situations.

Start small, begin with a manageable area, like a single room or even a specific area within a room. Tackling small sections makes the process less overwhelming. Do one room at a time. Divide items into categories such as keep, donate, sell, and discard. This helps in making decisions about each item. Setting realistic goals when decluttering. Whether it's cleaning out a closet, organizing a desk, or decluttering an entire room, setting realistic objectives helps maintain momentum.

The benefit of decluttering reduces stress, anxiety, and will give a clutter free environment. It can create a sense of calm and order, making it easier to relax and focus. A clutter-free workspace can enhance productivity. It allows for better concentration and reduces the time spent searching for items. One of the challenges of decluttering is letting go of items with sentimental value or those that evoke memories. It's important to strike a balance between keeping meaningful items and reducing unnecessary possessions. Decluttering can have emotional benefits, allowing individuals to detach from material possessions and focus on what truly matters.

A clear and organized space can stimulate creativity by providing a visually appealing and inspiring environment. With less clutter, it becomes easier to find things, resulting in more efficient use of time. Removing clutter reduces the risk of accidents and injuries by eliminating tripping hazards and improving overall safety in the living or working space.

Decluttering is not just for your household items but also your computer files as well. Decluttering extends to digital spaces as well. Organize files on your computer, clean up your email inbox, and review and delete digital content that is no longer necessary. After decluttering, it's important to develop habits that promote ongoing organization. Regularly assess and organize your belongings to prevent clutter from accumulating. Implementing a "one-in, one-out" rule can help maintain a clutter-free environment. For every new item brought in, consider removing one item.

There are three decluttering methods that I have tried in the past. The first is the KonMari Method. This method emphasizes organizing by category rather than location. It encourages individuals to assess each item's significance and keep only those that bring joy. Second is the 90/90 rule. If you haven't used an item in the last 90 days and don't foresee using it in the next 90 days, consider decluttering it. This rule is particularly applicable to clothing, gadgets, and other frequently used items. And last project 333. This minimalist fashion challenge involves selecting 33 items of clothing and accessories and wearing only those items for three months. It encourages a minimalist wardrobe and helps identify essential items. I haven't had much success with the first two, but Project 333 gave me much joy. I chose a ton of clothes that I haven't worn in a while and attempted to wear them but couldn't find a reason or use for them, so I sold them online. Those items I can no longer fit I kept thinking I was going to fit them someday. Well, that has opened a little more room in my closet. Since I am retired and stay at home in my garden, I don't need all those "club clothes" anymore.

Periodically reassess your possessions to prevent clutter from accumulating. Ask yourself if each item is still useful or brings joy. If not, consider letting it go. Use the change of seasons as an opportunity to declutter. Assess seasonal items, clothing, and decorations, and eliminate anything that is no longer needed or used. Cultivate habits that prevent clutter. For example, implement a nightly routine to tidy up living spaces, and practice the "one-in, one-out" rule when bringing new items into your home.

Decluttering is a personal and ongoing process that can lead to a more organized and peaceful living or working space. It's a journey that involves both physical and mental aspects, and finding a decluttering strategy that works for you is key to success. Whether adopting minimalist principles or simply organizing for practicality, the goal is to create a space that aligns with your values and promotes a sense of well-being.

Remember that decluttering is a personal journey, and there is no one-size-fits-all approach. It's about finding a method that resonates with you, fits your lifestyle, and contributes to a more organized and intentional way of living. Whether you're aiming for a minimalist lifestyle or simply seeking a more organized and stress-free space, the benefits of decluttering extend beyond the physical environment to positively impact mental and emotional well-being.

# Chapter 9:  Cutting Back

Get your finances organized by cutting back on things that you don't need first. This was a difficult task for me since I have a love for wine and hello kitty everything. I knew my spending habits were going to affect my finances.  Although I still buy that occasional hello kitty item and that bottle of wine. I will never tell you to stop buying that occasional coffee from Starbucks, but I will explain to you how to buy that coffee without breaking your budget.

So, you have your budget and still crave that coffee. What I have done, and it works for me. I created a way to make and sell something to get that bottle of wine or that hello kitty item. I use those apps I mentioned in a previous chapter to get that wine or that hello kitty item. Also, with my rewards and cashback on my credit cards I can get those items. I also have a no spend day once a week where I cannot spend any money no matter what. If it is a bill, I pay those all at the beginning of the month. What is left after my bills are paid, I take half of that and send to my investments. What is left I can use to buy something or take that and put towards my investments. It's my way of cutting back and giving back.

Cancel those subscriptions! Yes, with more and more magazines and books you can download for free, cancelling those unnecessary magazine subscriptions will save you a ton of money. Canceling all those subscriptions or memberships that you don't use frequently. This could include streaming services, gym memberships, or magazine subscriptions. Disconnecting from cable service can be difficult since we are at a time where everything is on TV. Utilize streaming channels such as Hulu, Netflix, or Disney. They have a lot of deals and if you are a college student you will get those streaming channels for a reduced price. Also bundling your services helps to save money.

Instead of going to expensive events or venues, look for free or low-cost entertainment options in your community, such as local parks, museums with free admission days, or community events.

Lower your energy bills by using energy-efficient appliances, turning off lights and electronics when not in use, and insulating your home to reduce heating and cooling costs. Save on water bills by fixing leaks, taking shorter showers, using a water-saving showerhead, and installing low-flow toilets. Be mindful of your water and electricity usage. Turn off lights and appliances when not in use and consider using natural light during the day.

If you use dryer sheets cut them in half. You can add days to your laundry. Don't wash on a half load, make sure your washer is full before starting. Consider buying second-hand clothing or participating in clothing swaps with friends. You can also extend the life of your current wardrobe by learning basic sewing skills to repair or alter your clothes.

Take preventive measures to stay healthy, such as exercising regularly and eating well, to reduce healthcare expenses in the long run. If you have space, consider growing your own fruits, vegetables, or herbs. This can help reduce your grocery expenses and provide you with fresh, organic produce.

If possible, use public transportation or carpool to save on gas and reduce wear and tear on your vehicle. This can also help you save on parking fees and maintenance costs. Cut back on driving by shopping online and having it delivered. Wal-Mart and Amazon have free shipping with prime service.

Instead of hiring professionals for every household repair or improvement, consider doing some tasks yourself. There are many tutorials available online for various DIY projects.

If you have high-interest debt, consider refinancing to lower your interest rates and reduce your monthly payments. This also helps in scaling down to a smaller house in retirement. If you have a spare room or a separate unit in your home, consider renting it out to generate extra income and offset your housing expenses. This will also help you to eliminate your debt.

When elevating life, you will need to take a critical look at your lifestyle and identify non-essential expenses, activities, or possessions that can be trimmed down or eliminated. Clarify your values and priorities. Focus on what truly brings you happiness and fulfillment and consider cutting back on activities or purchases that don't align with these values.

## Chapter 10: Meal Planning

Meal planning is the process of organizing and preparing meals in advance. It involves deciding what to eat for a set period, typically a week, and creating a corresponding grocery list. Meal planning offers several benefits, including saving time, reducing food waste, and promoting healthier eating habits. It also helps individuals stick to a budget and minimize the stress of deciding what to eat each day.

When meal planning, individuals typically consider factors such as dietary preferences, nutritional balance, and the convenience of preparation. They may also take into account any upcoming events or commitments that could impact on their meal schedule. By carefully selecting recipes and ingredients, individuals can streamline their cooking process and ensure they have the necessary items on hand.

Planning meals in advance saves time during the week. Knowing what to cook and having the necessary ingredients on hand reduces last-minute decision-making. Meal planning can be as simple as jotting down a few meal ideas for the week or as detailed as creating a comprehensive menu with corresponding recipes and shopping lists. It's a flexible process that can be tailored to fit individual preferences and lifestyles. This allows for strategic grocery shopping. By buying ingredients in bulk, taking advantage of sales, and minimizing food waste, you can save money in the long run. Planning meals enables you to make healthier food choices. You can incorporate a variety of nutritious ingredients and control portion sizes, leading to a balanced and well-rounded diet. The daily question of "What's for dinner?" can be stressful. Meal planning eliminates this uncertainty, reducing stress and making mealtimes more enjoyable.

Prepare meals at home rather than eating out. Cooking can be cost-effective, healthier, and allows you to control portion sizes. Plan your meals, buy in bulk, and consider batch cooking to save time and money.

Plan your meals by the week or monthly. We created a monthly menu for our meals. It does take time to create what you may want to eat each day. Since there are only two of us it is a bit easier to create. We don't really eat a lot during the day. Our breakfast is simple unless we desire something extra. Our dinner meals usually lasts two days, so our food budget is not high. We do grow our own vegetables and eat a lot of salads. We only eat two meals a day because we are always on the move.

Start this by outlining your week and identifying the days when you'll have more or less time to prepare meals. This can influence the complexity of the recipes you choose. Choose recipes based on your schedule, preferences, and nutritional goals. Consider incorporating a mix of familiar favorites and trying out new recipes. Once you've chosen your recipes, create a shopping list of all the ingredients you'll need. This helps prevent multiple trips to the store and ensures you have everything on hand. Take some time to wash, chop, and pre-portion ingredients when possible. This makes cooking during the week more efficient.

Make meal planning fun. Prepare larger quantities of certain dishes that can be portioned and stored for future meals. This is especially helpful for busy nights when you don't have time to cook from scratch. Assign a theme to each day of the week (e.g., pasta night, stir-fry night, meatless Monday). This adds variety and simplifies decision-making. Be flexible with your meal plan. Life can be unpredictable, and plans may change. Have a few backup options or quick recipes for busy days. Plan meals that can be repurposed into new dishes. For example, grilled chicken from one night can be used in a salad or wrap the next day.

There are various meal planning apps that can help you organize recipes, generate shopping lists, and even suggest meal ideas based on dietary preferences. Explore online platforms for meal inspiration and recipe ideas. Many websites allow you to save and organize your favorite recipes. Consider using kitchen gadgets like a slow cooker, instant pot, or air fryer to simplify meal preparation and save time. But be mindful of all the gadgets on the market. You don't want to create clutter anymore. So, look for something that can cook multiple meals. Overall, meal planning is a valuable tool for maintaining a well-balanced diet, saving time and money, and reducing the daily stress of meal preparation.

There are also meal planning kits you can order for you and your family. They are designed to meet your basic dietary needs. While most meals are designed to be prepared in a reasonable amount of time, some people may find that the cooking process still requires more time and effort than they're willing to invest.

Hello fresh is known for their flexibility and broad range of meal options. They also allow customers to choose from various plans based on dietary preferences. Blue Apron is one of the pioneers in the meal kit industry, offering a variety of recipes with pre-portioned ingredients. Sun Basket is another that focuses on organic and sustainably sourced ingredients, offering options for different dietary needs, including paleo, vegetarian, and Mediterranean. I found Home Chef to offer a variety of meal options with a particular emphasis on simplicity and customization. A new on the market is, "Plated". They provide chef-designed recipes with high-quality ingredients, allowing customers to choose from a diverse menu.

Meal planning kits can be a convenient solution for those seeking a balance between home-cooked meals and the convenience of pre-selected, pre-portioned ingredients. The industry has evolved over the years to address various preferences and concerns, making it important for consumers to choose a service that aligns with their values and meets their specific needs. But they can be costly over time. If you choose to use these services, make sure you add that into your monthly budget. Also include those days when you need more food for more family. While many services offer flexibility in terms of skipping weeks or changing meal selections, there might be limitations compared to complete freedom in traditional meal planning. As with the many services that offer flexibility in terms of skipping weeks or changing meal selections, there might be limitations compared to complete freedom in traditional meal planning.

If you or your family members have specific dietary preferences or restrictions, incorporate these considerations into your meal planning. This might include vegetarian or vegan options, gluten-free meals, or low-carb choices. Take into account any food allergies when planning meals, especially if cooking for a family or group.

Meal planning is a customizable process, and the key is finding a method that works for you. It can be as simple or detailed as you prefer, and the goal is to make mealtime more efficient, enjoyable, and aligned with your nutritional goals.

# Chapter 11: Environmental Stability

Consider investing in companies and funds that prioritize environmental and social responsibility. This can include investing in renewable energy, clean technology, sustainable agriculture, and companies with strong environmental and social governance (ESG) practices.

Support and invest in renewable energy sources such as solar, wind, and hydroelectric power. Investing in renewable energy technologies and supporting policies that promote their adoption can contribute to reducing greenhouse gas emissions and mitigating climate change. These investments not only contribute to a cleaner environment but can also offer long-term financial benefits as the demand for sustainable energy continues to grow.

Support organizations and initiatives focused on environmental conservation, wildlife protection, and sustainable land use. This can include investing in conservation funds or contributing to projects aimed at preserving natural habitats. Promote sustainable agricultural practices that prioritize soil health, water conservation, and biodiversity. Investing in sustainable agriculture initiatives can support the production of healthy food while minimizing environmental impact.

Incorporate sustainable practices into your daily life, such as reducing energy and water consumption, minimizing waste, supporting local and organic food producers, and choosing eco-friendly products.

By integrating sustainability into your investment decisions and lifestyle choices, you can contribute to positive environmental and social impact while potentially achieving long-term financial growth.

For some, frugal living can be motivated by a desire to live in a way that's more environmentally sustainable. By consuming fewer resources, minimizing waste, and choosing secondhand or eco-friendly options, individuals reduce their ecological footprint and contribute to a healthier planet. Embracing frugality often encourages individuals to become more self-reliant and resourceful. By learning to make do with less and finding creative solutions to everyday challenges, people can develop greater resilience in the face of financial or other uncertainties.

Environmental sustainability refers to the responsible use of natural resources to meet current needs without compromising the ability of future generations to meet their own needs. It involves making choices and adopting practices that minimize negative impacts on the environment, promote conservation, and support the overall well-being of the planet. This practice aims to reduce waste, minimize environmental impact, and promote long-term ecological balance.

Encourage conservation efforts and the preservation of natural habitats, biodiversity, and ecosystems. Supporting organizations and initiatives focused on environmental conservation can help protect valuable natural resources for future generations.

Transitioning from non-renewable energy sources (such as fossil fuels) to renewable sources (like solar). Environmental sustainability requires efforts to mitigate climate change by reducing greenhouse gas emissions. This involves transitioning to clean energy, improving energy efficiency, and adopting climate-friendly practices. In addition to mitigation, sustainability efforts also focus on adapting to the impacts of climate change. This includes building resilient infrastructure and communities that can withstand changing climatic conditions.

Sustainable water management involves using water efficiently in households, industries, and agriculture. This includes reducing water wastage, investing in water-saving technologies, and protecting water sources. Preventing water pollution and maintaining the quality of water bodies is crucial for environmental sustainability. This also includes proper disposal of pollutants and the protection of watersheds. Environmental sustainability includes efforts to protect and preserve natural ecosystems, promoting biodiversity. This involves conserving habitats, preventing deforestation, and combating the loss of species. Adopting sustainable agricultural practices, such as agroforestry and organic farming, helps maintain soil health, reduce chemical inputs, and promote biodiversity.

Minimizing waste generation and adopting responsible waste management practices are integral to environmental sustainability. This includes reducing, reusing, and recycling materials. This concept of a circular economy involves designing products with a focus on recycling and reusing materials, rather than a linear "take-make-dispose" model.

Environmental sustainability is a holistic concept that recognizes the interconnectedness of ecological, social, and economic systems. It requires a comprehensive and collaborative approach to address the challenges facing the planet and create a more resilient and balanced future. Individuals, communities, businesses, and governments all play crucial roles in advancing environmental sustainability.

Overall, it's a lifestyle that can promote financial stability, mindfulness, and a sense of freedom from the pressures of consumerism.

# Chapter 12: Frugal Tips

## Budgeting and Financial Planning:

Create a Budget: Develop a comprehensive budget that outlines your income, expenses, and savings goals. This provides a clear picture of your financial situation.

Track Expenses: Regularly monitor and analyze your spending habits to identify areas where you can cut back and save more.

Emergency Fund: Build and maintain an emergency fund to cover unexpected expenses, reducing the need to rely on credit cards or loans.

## Shop Smarter:

Buy in Bulk: Purchase non-perishable items, such as rice, pasta, and canned goods, in bulk to take advantage of lower unit prices.

Discount Stores: Explore discount grocery stores, warehouse clubs, or bulk food stores for cost-effective options on pantry staples.

Store Brands: Consider opting for store-brand or generic products, which are often more affordable than name-brand items.

Buy Generic Brands: Opt for store-brand or generic products, which are often more affordable than name-brand items without sacrificing quality.

Shop Sales and Clearance: Plan your purchases around sales, discounts, and clearance events to maximize savings on both essential and non-essential items.

Use Cashback Apps: Explore cashback apps and loyalty programs to earn rewards or cash back on everyday purchases.

**Plan Strategically:**

Seasonal Produce: Plan meals around seasonal produce, as it tends to be fresher and more affordable. Farmer's markets and local produce stands are excellent sources.

Sales and Specials: Base your meal plans on weekly sales and specials at your local grocery store. Adjust your recipes to incorporate discounted ingredients.

Meal Prep: Plan meals that use common ingredients to minimize waste and ensure everything in your grocery basket gets used.

**Minimize Food Waste:**

Use Leftovers Creatively: Repurpose leftovers into new meals to avoid food waste. For example, turn roasted vegetables into a frittata or use cooked chicken in a stir-fry.

Freeze Excess: If you have leftover ingredients, such as fresh herbs or bulk purchases, freeze them in portions for later use.

Compost: Consider starting a compost bin for food scraps to reduce the environmental impact of waste.

**DIY Convenience Foods:**

Homemade Sauces: Make your own sauces, dressings, and marinades. Not only is it often healthier, but it can also be more cost-effective than buying pre-packaged versions.

Prep Ingredients: Rather than buying pre-cut vegetables or pre-marinated meats, buy whole ingredients and prep them at home to save money.

Batch Cooking: Cook in batches and freeze portions for later use. This is especially helpful for busy days when cooking from scratch might be challenging.

**Explore Affordable Protein Sources:**

Plant-Based Proteins: Incorporate more plant-based protein sources, such as beans, lentils, and tofu, into your meals. These are often more budget-friendly than some animal proteins.

Economical Cuts: Choose less expensive cuts of meat and explore cooking methods that make them tender and flavorful.

### Optimize Leftovers:

Lunchbox Remix: Transform dinner leftovers into a delicious lunch for the next day. For example, turn grilled chicken into a sandwich or use roasted vegetables in a wrap.

Soup or Stew: Create a soup or stew with various leftovers, adding broth, spices, and additional vegetables for a tasty and thrifty meal.

### Reduce Eating Out:

Packed Lunch: Bring homemade lunches to work or school instead of buying food daily. This not only saves money but allows for better control over nutritional choices.

Dine-In Dinners: Instead of dining out, make restaurant-style meals at home. It's often more cost-effective, and you have control over ingredients and portions.

### Utilize Freezer and Pantry Staples:

Emergency Meals: Keep a stock of frozen vegetables, canned beans, and other pantry staples for quick, budget-friendly meals on busy days.

Freeze Extra: When you find a great deal on meat or produce, buy extra and freeze it for later use.

### DIY Snacks and Treats:

Snack Preparation: Make your own snacks, such as granola bars, popcorn, or trail mix, instead of purchasing pre-packaged versions.

Baking at Home: Bake treats and desserts at home. Homemade cookies, cakes, and muffins are often more affordable than store-bought alternatives.

## Community Resources:

Community Gardens: If available, participate in community gardens to access fresh produce at a lower cost.

Food Co-ops: Consider joining a food cooperative to purchase bulk items at discounted prices.

Swap Events: Participate in food swap events with friends or neighbors to exchange surplus garden produce, homemade goods, or pantry items.

## Embrace Minimalism:

Simplify Your Kitchen: Streamline your kitchen tools and gadgets to reduce clutter and focus on essentials. This can make meal preparation more efficient.

Mindful Consumption: Adopt a mindful approach to consumption, recognizing needs versus wants. This applies not only to food but also to kitchen equipment and accessories.

## DIY Cleaning Products:

Homemade Cleaners: Create your own cleaning products using common household items like vinegar and baking soda. This is not only cost-effective but also environmentally friendly.

Reusable Cleaning Cloths: Use washable and reusable cleaning cloths instead of disposable options to save money in the long run.

## Thrifty Meal Planning:

Meal Prep: Plan meals for the week, prep ingredients in advance, and batch-cook to save time and money.

Brown-Bag Lunch: Bring homemade lunches to work or school to avoid the cost of eating out daily.

Shop with a List: Stick to a grocery shopping list to avoid impulse purchases and focus on necessities.

## Reduce Utilities and Household Expenses:

Energy Efficiency: Implement energy-saving practices, such as turning off lights and appliances when not in use, using energy-efficient light bulbs, and maintaining home insulation.

Cut Cable: Explore alternatives to cable TV, such as streaming services or digital antennas, to reduce entertainment costs.

Negotiate Bills: Regularly review and negotiate bills for services like internet, insurance, and subscriptions to ensure you're getting the best rates.

## Mindful Transportation:

Carpooling: Consider carpooling or ride sharing to save on fuel costs and reduce vehicle wear and tear.

Public Transportation: Use public transportation whenever possible to cut down on fuel and parking expenses.

Biking or Walking: Choose biking or walking for short-distance trips to save on transportation costs and promote a healthy lifestyle.

## DIY and Repurposing:

Repurpose Clothing: Update and repurpose old clothing through simple alterations or by turning them into new items like rags or reusable bags.

DIY Home Repairs: Learn basic home repair skills to handle minor fixes without the need for professional assistance.

Homemade Cleaners: Make your own cleaning products using simple and cost-effective ingredients like vinegar and baking soda.

## Embrace Secondhand and Thrift Shopping:

Thrifting: Explore thrift stores, consignment shops, and online platforms for secondhand items, including clothing, furniture, and household goods.

Garage Sales and Flea Markets: Attend garage sales and flea markets to find unique items at lower prices.

Online Marketplace: Utilize online marketplaces to buy and sell gently used items, reducing the need for new purchases.

**Minimalism and Decluttering:**

Quality Over Quantity: Prioritize quality over quantity when making purchases, focusing on items that serve a purpose and bring long-term value.

Declutter Regularly: Regularly declutter your living space to minimize unnecessary possessions and prevent impulse buying.

Mindful Consumption: Before making a purchase, ask yourself if it aligns with your values and if you genuinely need the item.

**Frugal Entertainment:**

Free and Low-Cost Activities: Explore free community events, parks, libraries, and other low-cost entertainment options.

DIY Entertainment: Create your own entertainment, such as hosting game nights, movie nights at home, or exploring outdoor activities.

Library Resources: Take advantage of your local library for books, movies, and educational resources at no cost.

**Financial Education:**

Continuous Learning: Invest time in learning about personal finance, budgeting, and investing to make informed financial decisions.

Financial Literacy Resources: Utilize free or low-cost financial literacy resources, including online courses, books, and educational websites.

Seek Professional Advice: If needed, consider consulting with a financial advisor for personalized guidance on managing your finances.

**Frugal Socializing:**

Potluck Gatherings: Host potluck dinners or gatherings where each guest brings a dish, reducing the overall cost.

Explore Free Events: Attend free community events, outdoor concerts, or festivals for entertainment without a hefty price tag.

Volunteer Together: Engage in volunteer activities with friends, combining socializing with community service.

**Mindful Health and Wellness:**

Home Workouts: Exercise at home using free workout videos or apps, eliminating the need for a gym membership.

Preventive Healthcare: Prioritize preventive healthcare measures, such as a healthy diet and regular exercise, to reduce long-term medical expenses.

Generic Medications: Opt for generic medications when available to save on prescription costs.

# CONCLUSION

Frugal living encourages resourcefulness and adaptability, traits that can be valuable in retirement. By embracing simple living and a mindset focused on needs over wants, retirees may find it easier to adjust their lifestyles to changing financial circumstances. By avoiding unnecessary expenses, individuals may have more flexibility in their choices and experiences. This could include the ability to pursue non-traditional career paths, take sabbaticals, or retire earlier than planned.

You can do this by changing how you view your money. Learning the basics of wants and needs will help you in retirement. Focus on what matters in your life such as family, living life to its fullest. A frugal lifestyle encourages individuals to evaluate their priorities and focus on what truly matters to them. This can lead to a more fulfilling life by emphasizing experiences, relationships, and personal growth over material possessions. By avoiding unnecessary expenses, individuals may have more flexibility in their choices and experiences. This could include the ability to pursue non-traditional career paths, take sabbaticals, or retire earlier than planned.

Remember that financial stability in retirement is an ongoing process that requires periodic review and adjustments. Life circumstances, economic conditions, and personal goals may change, necessitating modifications to your retirement plan to ensure continued financial security. Overall, frugal living can play a significant role in helping individuals save for retirement, maintain financial stability during your retirement years, and potentially achieve greater peace of mind and independence as you age.